AF422850

praise for
HEARTS

Finding Unexpected Signs *of* Hope, Comfort, *and* Joy

"This book speaks to finding grace and comfort in knowing that true love can be gifted, from one person to another. Words express it, as do deeds and actions. Roze speaks of gifting others with what you do, what you say, how you act and react with simple acts of kindness."

—Mike London, Head Football Coach William & Mary

"Roze Worrell's extraordinary 'heart-finds' are proof-positive of the guidance, comfort, and love available to us—when our hearts and minds are open."

—Constance Costas, former editor-in-chief, *Virginia Living* magazine

"*HEARTS: Finding Unexpected Signs of Hope, Comfort, and Joy* serves as a powerful reminder that God's presence permeates our lives, if only we pause to recognize Him. As a veteran, I view this book as a mosaic of beautiful heart-inspired images and short stories, capable of uplifting the spirits of fellow veterans struggling with depression and PTSD, and guiding them towards inspiration, hope, and ultimately God's healing embrace."

—Frank Cucci, Former U.S. Navy SEAL and CEO of Linxx Global, Inc.

"Finally, a book that is profound in its simplicity, elegant in its execution, and life changing in its effect. *HEARTS* is a little book with a powerful message of hope and connection in our world that is struggling to find its way. You will find little wonders, happy coincidences, and an overwhelming sense that you are not alone in this world."

—Christopher Hoye III, MBA, United States Marshal

"This book has a heartfelt way of fostering hope, magnifying faith, and confirming love. It has nuggets of truth for everyone and is an easy read that you will not want to put down. Roze's book is also a testament to a mother's enduring love. Because she flawlessly reveals her innermost thoughts and feelings, it sparks readers toward their own introspection."

—The Honorable Eileen A. Olds
Retired Judge and Author of *Twin Expectations: Raising the Bar, Raising Expectations, Raising Children!*

"Today, more than ever, we need God's presence in our lives. *HEARTS: Finding Unexpected Signs of Hope, Comfort, and Joy* serves as an inspirational reminder of how meaningful and fulfilled our lives can be "when we're open to God's presence and support, we can be at peace in our hearts and minds." Roze has a way of reaching out and touching everyone with her personal reflections."

—Tony DiClemente, Deputy Assistant Director, FBI (retired)

HEARTS

Finding Unexpected
Signs *of*
Hope,
Comfort,
and
Joy

Roze Worrell

Published by Little Star
Richmond, VA

This is a work of non-fiction and contains the author's personal recollections and reflections of experiences over time. Events and timelines have been compressed and emotions explored.
Contact the author at rozeworrell.com

ISBN 979-8-9861299-4-5

Book and cover design by Wendy Daniel Design
The hearts on the cover and in the book are photos of Roze Worrell's heart-finds. A few are included in this book; many will be featured on Roze's website. Visit www.rozeworrell.com to follow along.

Printed in the United States of America
To reduce environmental impact, this book is produced on uncoated paper and in small batches.

You have always believed in me
and supported me. Thank you from the
bottom of my heart for never giving up
on me getting my book published.
It's your loving heart that keeps mine beating.

♥ ♥ ♥

Author's Note

My book shares some of my many amazing heart-finds and the stories behind them. These unexpected treasures come in all sizes and textures: some simple and rustic, others popping in silver and gold and an array of colors, especially pastels. The photos of these finds are unedited images taken with my phone. I chose to print them without enhancement or edit to retain the authentic and serendipitous nature of each find.

There's such a natural beauty and power in the simplicity of each one. For me, they feel like whispers of encouragement—reminders of a divine presence that surrounds us. I can feel God's embrace and the hearts' gentle nudges telling me that despite my challenges and hardships, everything is going to be okay. But this isn't a book about convincing you of my beliefs. It's simply an invitation to share these awe-inspiring hearts in hopes that they will lift you up as they do me. Consider my story an ode to the extraordinary hidden in the ordinary. My wish is to spark feelings of wonder and splendor in our glorious universe.

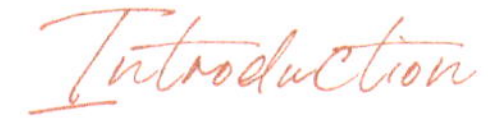

sharing my heart

"Peace is the harmony of the mind and the heart."

—Thich Nhat Hanh

For some, it's butterflies or ladybugs. For others, it's cardinals. As for me, I feel God's presence and hear his messages of encouragement and assurance with hearts.

I believe that we're not alone. We just need to be tuned in. Fewer than 24 hours after I declared the heart with outreached hands to be my life symbol, I came across a rock, perfectly shaped like a heart, while hiking the San Juan Mountains of southwestern Colorado.

In that instant, I knew God was telling me I had chosen the right guidepost for my life. That was over 40 years ago. Ever since, I've been finding the most extraordinary hearts. Better yet, they have been finding me!

God's presence is all around us. Whether we're on top of the world or at the end of our rope, He is always providing affirmation and inspiration. *HEARTS: Finding Unexpected Signs of Hope, Comfort, and Joy* is a compilation of my incredible heart-finds accompanied by my reflections and insights and paired with powerful quotes. At any time, you can flip to any page and feel understood and emboldened, for when we're open to God's presence and support, we can be at peace in our hearts and minds. Our faith will be reinforced, and hope, comfort, and joy will embrace us.

I hope this little book of my personal reflections and insights along with my heart treasures will be a feast for your eyes and a balm for your soul. My incredible heart-finds, both nature-made and man-made that I have happened upon while going about my daily life, have given me a sense of peace, strength, and well-being. I'm hopeful they will touch your heart, renew your faith, make you smile, give you strength, and inspire you beyond measure.

finding my heart

"When you open your heart to receive, the universe will shower you with gifts."

—Unknown

Who in their right mind would want to sweat it out in the Colorado Rockies for 23 days with very little sleep, food (no caffeine or sweets to boot), and minimal protection from snow, rain, hail, cold, and heat? Me! To my father's dismay and puzzlement, I decided to take a survival course after I graduated from college, before I started my first real job.

I had been through a lot of ups and downs during my four years in college, the biggest being the death of my mom in March of 1981, toward the end of my third year. She was only 46 years old, but in the over 20 years I'd had the privilege to be her daughter, she became the most influential person in my life. She was incredibly smart and talented and simply did not know the meaning of "It can't be done." She was a wonderful mother to four girls, served as the office manager for my father's law practice, read the law under his tutelage, and passed the bar on her first attempt. She was amazing in my eyes and to all who had the good fortune to cross paths with her. Her actions encouraged me to be the best I could be and to never ever give up. Having to watch her courageous—but unsuccessful—battle with cancer, her approval and respect for the decisions I made in life were of utmost importance. On the day of her funeral, my father called me upstairs to their bedroom, reached into his suit jacket pocket and handed me a necklace. It wasn't just any necklace. It was the Tiffany Elsa Peretti rose-gold open-heart necklace he had given to my mom on Valentine's Day, less than a month before she passed away. He knew when he gave it to her that she wasn't coming home. She was at Memorial Sloan Kettering in New York City, where she had been for over six weeks. He told me she had held the necklace in her hands while tears streamed down her face. She never wore it. I was speechless. He told me he wanted me to have the necklace for all I had done for my mom and the family while she was sick. For my father to recognize my efforts when he was going through so much turmoil and heartache was unfathomable. For him to want me to have something so special, something he thoughtfully picked out and gave to my mom, was equally difficult to absorb. It was the gift of all gifts; it meant the world. Little did I know that this heart necklace was the foreshadowing of something just as amazing that would occur in my life 15 months later.

So, when I graduated from college in May of 1982, I was hell-bent on taking a survival course. Having tried to deal with the issues that cropped up from my mother passing away when I was so young—before graduation, marriage, or success in the real world—it seemed right for me to have this introspective experience. Whether I was escaping from the realities of life or trying to understand them, I truly believed this survival course would fill the bill. I knew I needed to do it so much that I advised my first post-college employer, the Dow Chemical Company in Los Angeles, that I would start a month later than they suggested. I had no clue what would come from it all, but something in my heart and soul told me this was the path I needed to take.

Who has ever heard of a snowfall in the month of June? Or, who from the South, who has never traveled west of Virginia, has heard of a snowfall in the month of June? Well, there I was, on the 16th of June in 1982, in one of the most beautiful parts of the country, the West San Juan Mountains of the Colorado Rockies. I signed up for what I imagined to be a once-in-a-lifetime experience, a 23-day course, offered by Outward Bound, that promised to be challenging physically, mentally, and emotionally. From mountain climbing, glissading, and fording rivers to technical rock climbing and rappelling, I was going to do things I had never done before, and my father thought it was the craziest graduation gift he had ever heard of. But this is what I wanted to do before I entered the working world. Never in my wildest dreams did I expect to trek through snow or to have to actually wear an ice helmet. I figured the helmet was just some precautionary measure the attorneys required the instructors to distribute. Those of us who had brought long johns were told to leave them behind so only the most necessary items would take up space in our backpacks. But on the first day of the course, snow decided to greet us in a big way. Not only did I not have the appropriate clothing for it, I had very little experience getting around in it. My only experience with snow was limited to the handful of times during my childhood where school was closed because of just a few inches. Of course, those few inches not only seemed like so much more, but they were magical in my eyes, and not just because I didn't have to go to school.

I was out of my element, yet I thought that this whole snow thing would be a piece of cake. Boy, was I ever wrong. I remember quite vividly trying to learn how to posthole and traverse these very steep mountain sides covered in no less than a foot of snow. Although I didn't think I would have a physical problem getting where I needed to go, it became quite obvious my biggest obstacle was mental—my fear of failure. So imagine my embarrassment when I fell on my butt over and over again, which then got me off course because of the subsequent sliding. I kept thinking, "How am I supposed to make a good first impression with these nine people I've been grouped with just a few hours ago?" The last thing I wanted to do was to look either weak or incompetent—or worse—both.

Another challenge with the course was food and drink. I had to go without two things that had always been staples in my diet—diet soda and sweets. A day without something sweet was like a day without air—it was that essential. I had acquired a taste for diet sodas as far back as the fifth grade when my school offered us Tab and salted peanuts, which my female classmates and I would pour into our soda before indulging. In the mountains, the only liquid we had was good 'ol H2O with a catch. We had to spike it with iodine because of the risk of dysentery or some kind of bacterial infection. In no time, quenching my frequent thirst far outweighed the quirky taste of the water. There were only a few sweet things in our diet, and one was Wyler's lemonade mix. I have always been a lover of sweet, tart, lemony things, so the Wyler's was a huge treat. But we didn't have much—rationing was a must. We took turns sticking our fingers in the green and yellow tin can for a lick, and sometimes we would mix the granules with snow.

I remember the day some of the guys were horsing around and dropped the can, causing all of what remained to spill to the ground. I was not happy. They had dropped our magic elixir. There was no way I was going to let that mix go to waste, so I knelt to the ground licking up as much of the mix as I could.

As for food, I had never been much of a breakfast eater, but I knew I would be an idiot not to fuel my engine if I wanted to survive each day's challenges. Unfortunately, the breakfast was a thick and gooey oatmeal that would typically be very difficult for me to get down my throat. But after waking up to frigid temps and an empty stomach and having to put on ice-cold hiking boots, lumpy oatmeal took on a surprising appeal.

On day seven of the course, we re-supplied our gear and food and shared more of ourselves with each other. We were asked to identify our "life symbol." At the ripe age of 21, I didn't have a life symbol, but I gave it a whole lot of thought and decided it would be a heart with a hand reaching out from each side. I socked the exercise away in my heart and mind, so I could focus on the next physical hurdle.

On day eight, we had to trek up a steep mountain with a magnificent waterfall cascading down its majestic crevices. At that point in time, however, I was incapable of taking in all the beauty of my surroundings. The first seven days, I had eaten things I would not normally eat, had come across snow storms I had not been prepared for, used muscles I didn't know I had, and cherished every bit of shut eye I could get, knowing the next day was going to be equally, if not more difficult than the day I had just completed. To put it simply, I was tired, sore, dirty, hungry, and more than a bit grouchy. To make matters much worse, I was carrying 70 pounds of supplies and personal effects on my back with a pack that had a fixed suspension. It was impossible to evenly distribute the 70 pounds. Bottom line, I was only thinking about getting my butt to the top of the mountain. The life symbol I had just chosen for myself the day before was certainly not on my mind.

As I slowly but surely made it up the rocky mountain terrain, my knees were more strained, and my face was closer to the ground than I would have liked. As I was trying to push through and focus on how great I would feel when I got to the top, a rock caught my eye. There it was, nestled among thousands, if not millions, of other rocks with clumps of dirt and slivers of ice. It was a stone like no other—perfectly shaped like a heart. There were an astronomical number of rocks on this mountain, and yet this particular one found me. I felt God was giving me a sign that I had chosen the right life symbol. He was affirming that I was supposed to take this course, be on this mountain, and have that rock find me the day after I had declared my life symbol. I knew I couldn't go wrong in life if I kept my faith and let my heart lead me.

Consequently, the heart has been an integral part of my life for over 40 years, and, along with my faith and my mind, serves as my life's compass.

This book shares some of my many incredible heart-finds that have unexpectedly given me the lift I so needed at particular moments. I believe they are messages from God letting me know He's with me, providing hope, comfort, and joy. No matter what we're going through or worried about, steadfast faith can inspire and reassure us. With it, we are able to connect to inner peace and true happiness, and realize that everything is going to be okay.

opening my heart

"When you write from the heart, you not only light the dark path of your readers, you light your own way as well."

—Marjorie Powers

I'm an open book except for the deeply personal chapters I keep locked away, hidden even from myself. These experiences are so raw, so deeply personal, that they trigger an emotional struggle not just with the thought of sharing them but when my mind wanders there as well. But as I was writing *HEARTS*, I realized a truth: I must share the most painful story in order for you to better understand me, my journey, and my connection with the heart. The heart necklace my father gave me the day we buried my mother, the one he had given my mom less than a month before she died, immediately became my most prized material possession. To hear my dad express his appreciation meant the world. While I was dealing with the worst event in my young life, his gift made me feel that his love could help me endure and carry on.

Although my dad was an upbeat and fun-loving father, I learned how much he struggled with painful emotions a few weeks before my mom died. I hadn't seen her in over a month. My father gave me no warning of what to expect, and I had no idea how I would react. I was overwhelmed with emotion when my eyes locked in on hers and I saw how much she had deteriorated in such a short period of time. She could no longer talk, but her eyes still spoke to me. My dad wouldn't allow any tears. His reaction to mine not only upset me more but also scared the daylights out of me. He told me to get out of the room, that there would be no crying around my mom. I could understand why he didn't want my mom seeing me upset, but I was so hurt and confused by his intense anger. As the years went by after her death, I came to understand that his outburst was about my mom losing her battle with her cancer, despite the Herculean efforts she had made with his support, as well as his inability to handle my inconsolable grief, and his own as well. But in that moment, I was hurt and guilt ridden, thinking I had disappointed him.

This visit with my mom was my last before she died.

As painful as it is to commit the rest of the story to paper, I truly believe opening up about this heartache will help reader and writer alike. I lost my mother's necklace seven years after my dad gave it to me and six years after I proclaimed the heart with two hands to be my life symbol. It's hard to describe how heavily this has weighed on me. For quite some time, a wave of guilt and remorse would come over me when my mind went there, so much so that oftentimes, I couldn't keep from welling up. Until now, only a handful of people have known about this. I didn't even have the courage to tell my dad I lost it, and he lived until 2021, 40 years after my mom's passing. I thought about telling him many times, but my anxiety over what his reaction might be prevented me.

I've always embraced my heart-finds' positive messages from up above, but what took significant time was accepting them as messages of grace from God and my mom, one of his angels. It has always been obvious that my heart-shaped treasures are God's way of giving me hope, comfort, and joy, but I had to work on giving myself grace. And once I got comfortable with that, it was evident to me that my heart-finds were also messages of grace from above. For way too long, I carried a burden of guilt, imagining my mom's hurt and disappointment in me for losing the necklace. But now, when I come upon a heart, I not only feel pure happiness and peace, I'm assured that God and my mom have been telling me for years that it's okay. Neither are upset with me; they know the loss wasn't deliberate. This realization lifted a huge weight and ensured a profound and constant peace of mind and heart.

It is my sincere hope that my story can help you with yours and that it will inspire you to give yourself compassion. I know all too well how hard it is to not beat yourself up over something you wish had never happened. The guilt and stress we take on can be debilitating. But we must remember that God knows our intentions and gives us His love and inspiration. If we keep ourselves open, He and his angels will guide us through our struggles and encourage us to focus the energy of our hearts on our blessings and to dedicate our time to cherishing them.

Finding hearts isn't something I ever actively set out to do; it's never been a conscious practice. My heart-finds hold a special significance because of their serendipitous nature. I surmise that because of those two fateful days (day 7 when I declared my life symbol and day 8 when I came upon my amazing heart rock) during the survival course in 1982, my mind is attuned to seeing heart shapes everywhere, but I also know that the heart-shaped rocks, puddles, charms, earrings, trinkets and trees have nothing to do with my mind. Regardless, I consider them unexpected heavenly gifts, like the heart rock. They appear before me when I'm just going about my day—whether I'm checking my post office box, shopping, driving, taking a walk, mowing the lawn, or rushing out of the rain to get in my husband's truck. They're waiting to be discovered, always lifting me up and keeping me going.

While hearts resonate deeply with me, I realize they may not have the same profound meaning for you. Something else may speak to you. It could be a dragonfly or a rainbow. The key is to be open to these signs—special nudges from God, giving us fortitude and inspiration.

"What we have once enjoyed we can never lose. All that we love deeply becomes a part of us."

—Helen Keller

present for broken hearts

I don't know many people who look forward to going to visitations and funerals, but we often attend them as a way to show our love and support for the surviving family.

Recently, my husband and I went to a visitation for the father of someone he worked with many years ago. His old colleague hasn't lived in our area for many years, but when he did, we would occasionally get together with him and his wife. I enjoyed their company, and I especially enjoyed his wife. Although my husband has only had occasional contact with his old colleague over the years, he has always appreciated their past working relationship. He has a much harder time going to funerals and visitations than I do, and this one was no exception. But I knew in my heart we should go, and when I reminded him of why I thought it would mean so much to his old work buddy, he totally got it.

It turns out I was spot on, and I also had the joy of reconnecting with the wife. But what also lifted me up and reinforced my positive feelings about our attendance was this amazing heart I came upon when we were leaving the funeral home. I didn't see it when we arrived, but it sure caught my attention when we were walking back to our car to go home. I could feel God letting me know he was with us, and we had done the right thing.

It's so important to be there for those we care about when they are grieving. It not only helps heal their hearts, but it makes ours feel so full.

"There is no exercise better for the heart than reaching down and lifting people up."

—John Holmes

affirmation

I had a choice to eat more brownies or cut into my kiwi. I chose to have the kiwi. Evidently, this was the right choice. Such a delightful surprise!

"Once you make a decision, the universe conspires to make it happen."

—Anne Frank

hope and possibility

This particular find looks like a heart-shaped balloon with mini hearts spraying from it, but it's actually some kind of oil spill on a neighborhood street.

Typically, balloons are associated with celebrations of joyous events in our work lives like promotions and retirements, and in our personal lives like birthdays and engagements, all of which make our hearts happy. On a deeper level, balloons symbolize our aspirations or our desires to let go of whatever may be holding us back. Either way, these fragile, air-filled, colorful vessels can have a huge positive impact on our hearts.

"Your life is like a balloon. If you never let yourself go, you will never know how far you can rise."

—Linda Poindexter

always be gentle

Life is such a wonderful gift each of us is given. And there are times when we feel so content and lucky to be where we are and have what we have. We cherish those times' special touchstones. But there are very challenging times as well, such that we need to dig deep and find our inner strength to face the day and tackle the hurdles that lie ahead. We have the battle scars to prove it.

This lovely weathered heart-shaped flower petal caught my eye and reinforced how much of an impact the tough times can have on our lives. And we are all fragile even though it may not be as visibly apparent with some as it is with others.

We need to always be kind and gentle with each other. At the very least, treat everyone the way we hope everyone will treat us.

"If we could look into each other's hearts and understand the unique challenges each of us faces, I think we would treat each other much more gently, with more love, patience, tolerance, and care."

—Marvin J. Ashton

survive and thrive

Have you ever said, "I feel like I've been hit by a Mack truck?" I'll admit I've said this from time to time, but I typically only say it to my ride or die, my husband. And I've said it because I've had more than I can handle physically, emotionally, or mentally.

It's normal for all of us to feel like this at one time or another. When I get to this point, I know I need to slow down and try to take care of myself. Knowing this is easy, but actually doing it can be a challenge.

"Put your heart, mind, and soul
into even your smallest acts.
This is the secret of success."

—Swami Savananda

never lose hope

I will be the first to admit that I have days when I feel overwhelmed or discouraged. At these times, I can't shut off my brain, worrying about my loved ones' declining health or about my projects that aren't progressing as I think they should. I find myself thinking about them constantly and feeling helpless.

If any of you ever feel this way, I not only can empathize, but I'm here for you.

This recent funky heart-find with all of its cracks, crevices, and blemishes not only reminds us of how our tough days make us feel, but it also gives us strength and hope. Despite all the unknowns, trials, and setbacks in our lives, we can't lose hope. Keeping faith in our hearts will enable us to persevere, cope, and succeed.

"Faith means living with uncertainty —
feeling your way through life,
letting your heart guide you
like a lantern in the dark."

—Dan Millman

"To live in hearts we leave behind
is not to die."

—Thomas Campbell

no fear

A very dear long-time friend's obituary was in yesterday's paper. I have known him since elementary school. Although I knew his passing was imminent, it hit me hard. He was only 61 years young.

In his last few months, we spoke, but not as much as we exchanged texts. I loved and respected the person he was. He had a very strong faith in God, and when we communicated, he never hesitated to tell me exactly what he thought on a variety of topics. He wasn't one to mince his words.

About three months ago, he went skydiving tandem style. He described it as "... my lifetime dream. I had absolutely no fear... none! It felt completely like I met my destiny." He sent me lots of photos. I could feel his excitement and pure joy.

This recent heart-find immediately reminded me of my friend because it looks like a butterfly (I'm pretty sure it's actually an old poinsettia) and because of his exhilarating skydiving experience. It's the perfect heart to memorialize him. Having always heard the butterfly symbolizes life after this life and new beginnings, and recalling his absolute thrill when he fulfilled his dream to skydive, it seems so fitting.

You will always have a special place in my heart, John.

feeling the feels

Have you ever been in a parking lot and debated how you're going to navigate it? Yesterday, that's exactly what happened to me. Something told me to take one path over another, and bam, I see this incredible heart!

At first, I thought it was a penny because of its color. And as I got closer, I still thought it was a penny that somehow was bent into the shape of a heart, but then I realized it was a lovely old heart charm with a tiny bonus heart embossed on top.

After a little digging, I learned that the inscription says, "I love you" in several different languages. But what I knew immediately is that this heart-find brought me incredible joy and peace, and it's so important to soak up the positive feelings in our hearts.

"Enjoy the little things in life, for
one day you may look back and
realize they were the big things."

—Robert Brault

God's embrace

You're looking at the path in our neighborhood that leads to a couple of docks on the Lafayette River. On any given day, you can launch a kayak, canoe, or paddle board from one of these docks. The path is quite worn from all who frequent it. I have launched my kayak from here, but I especially enjoy going out to one of the docks to soak in the river's beauty. It always has a way of comforting my mind and soothing my heart.

Can you see what recently caught my eye as I was walking towards one of the docks? I've made this trek more times than I can count, but this was the first time I noticed how a patch of the ground formed a heart. As you can imagine, I was overcome with joy before I even got to the dock. It was as if God was welcoming me to my little slice of heaven.

We all need a safe place—a place where we can protect ourselves from all the chaos going on around us.

"We should all find a quiet place, a peaceful space, to bury the chaos and rest for a while."

—Christy Ann Martine

hope is where the heart is

I can't help but think I crossed paths with this heart rock, standing out in a bed of endless rocks, for a reason. We're in the last week of December, and I've been contemplating what may be in store for us in the new year.

This bold heart rock is a nod from God to remain hopeful for a healthy and peaceful year.

This beautiful heart-find has so much character and strength; it looks to have weathered many a storm, reflective of all the ups and downs life throws at us.

No matter how tough things have been, there's always hope.

"God speaks to us in many ways, but sometimes we miss the signs He sends us. Be open to receiving His messages of hope, and your heart will be filled with joy."

—Unknown

not always obvious

The day after Halloween, I expected to come across random candy wrappers and even candy dropped from trick-or-treaters' goody bags. But as you can imagine, I was so surprised and excited to come upon this heart-shaped costume jewelry earring. I found it face down. When I turned it over, I discovered it had a striking heart-shaped black onyx encased in gemstones as its centerpiece. And its ear clasp was a delicate cluster of five tiny interconnected hearts.

Like all my heart-finds, this one has given me much joy and reinforced my awareness of God being ever present in my life. It also reminded me that God's signs don't have to be found in nature; they can appear in a variety of ways, but they all provide me with a sense of security and inner peace.

God is always with us. Some signs are more obvious than others. We just need to keep our hearts and minds open.

"If you can find Him in everything,
you won't miss Him in anything."
—Peter Mattis

"In any given moment we have two
options: to step forward into growth
or to step back into safety."

—Abraham Maslow

take the steps

This unique heart-find came into view when I was being careful not to trip as I took a step off an uneven curb. I'm not sure what it's made of. It appears to be pieces of a broken shell. Regardless, it's definitely a heart. And when I got home and looked more closely at my photo, I noticed a charming little heart on top of the initial big one.

There have been things in my personal and work life I haven't pursued or pursued with hesitation because I feared the end result would not be good enough. The truth is, I let my fears keep me from taking the steps I needed to take. Even though I knew I needed to just do it, I allowed my negative internal thoughts to hold me back.

Call me crazy, but these two hearts not only give me pure joy, but I believe there's a reason I found them or they found me. God is always with me and believes in me. And if I don't believe in myself, how can I expect others to?

We all need to let go of our inhibitions and take the necessary steps to accomplish the things we're fearful of doing.

> "Don't be pushed around by the fears in your mind. Be led by the dreams in your heart."
>
> —Roy T. Bennett

beauty in the everyday

There's no denying I have always struggled with our extremely hot and humid summer days here in Virginia. They have a way of zapping so much of my energy. By the time I walk from my house to my car, I often feel like a wilted flower.

But as I get up in age, I realize it's so important to earnestly focus on all the good things in my life, to not lose sight of all the beauty God creates each and every day, regardless of the season.

Look at this beautiful pink crape myrtle! Either by foot or car, I typically go by this tree several times a week, but today, I actually saw its lovely heart-shaped crown. I was in such awe of God's amazing creation that the sweltering weather escaped my mind.

We're surrounded by so many heavenly gifts. Let's not take them for granted.

"Never lose an opportunity of seeing anything that is beautiful; for beauty is God's handwriting—a wayside sacrament. Welcome it in every fair face, in every fair sky, in every fair flower, and thank God for it as a cup of blessing."

—Ralph Waldo Emerson

heart smile

I'll bet I'm not the only person who has gone to the grocery store and been shopping for a while, only to suddenly realize the coupons were left in the car.

When I'm alone and this happens, it's not as stressful because I'm only inconveniencing myself. But recently, on an extremely hot and humid day in July, this occurred when my husband was accompanying me. And he's typically ready to leave the store as soon as we get there. So, it wasn't surprising that he told me to forget about the coupons when I told him what I had done. As much as I like to please everyone, especially my husband, it didn't dissuade me from wanting to get those coupons.

I bolted back to the car that was, unfortunately, nowhere near the store's entrance. And look what was smiling at me in the space next to our vehicle — amazing!

A comforting nod from the universe. It affirmed my decision to dash back to the car for the coupons. It may seem trivial to most, but it meant so much to me. A feeling of peace came over me. Such a powerful reminder of divine presence in my life and the support it provides me.

—Charles Spurgeon

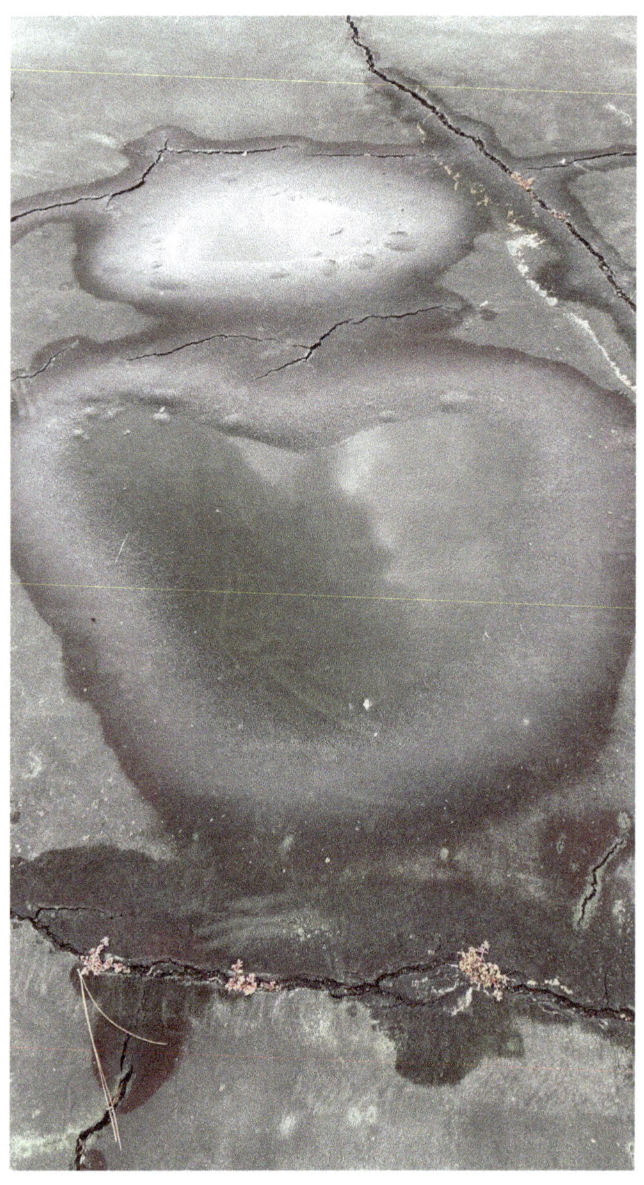

weathered and lovely

This heart-find is so cool and unusual. Interestingly, it's on a city tennis court I used to play on many, many years ago. The court brings back a multitude of special memories.

As much as I love how the rain left this unique heart, I was sad to see all the court's cracks, mold, and weeds. Obviously, the court hasn't received much attention, if any, in quite some time.

Seeing the heart juxtaposed with the unattended tennis court, I couldn't help but be reminded that just because something or someone is weathered or old doesn't mean, they have lost any of their heart or worth; and no matter how aged something or someone is, they still need love and attention.

"Do all the good you can,
By all the means you can,
In all the ways you can,
In all the places you can,
At all the times you can,
To all the people you can,
As long as ever you can."

—John Wesley

tiny droplet

I noticed this precious droplet of water on our kitchen sink while doing the dishes. A very unexpected but oh-so-welcome heart-find.

It reminds me of how delicate our lives are. We can never lose sight of the impact our words and actions have, however brief and small they may be.

"Penetrate the heart of just one drop of water, and you will be flooded by a hundred oceans."

—Mahmûd Shabistarî

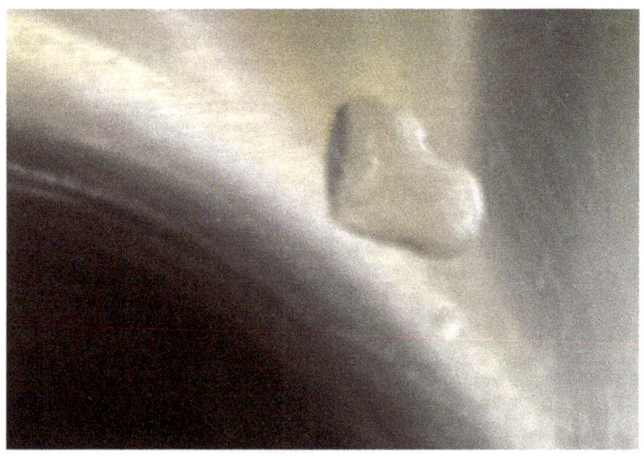

endless possibilities

What a wonderful day! It's the first day of winter—my favorite season—and look what I found this morning in a Norfolk parking lot. It's a small plastic light bulb with, of course, a heart.

When our hearts and minds are open, the possibilities are limitless. Let's always keep the light on in both of them!

"When you possess light within, you see it externally."

—Anais Nin

mind's eye

I came upon this unique heart-find on my way to the post office. At first glance, I saw this raised heart with some very sharp defining edges. But after I took my phone out to take a photo and focus on what I thought was a heart, I could see that the beautiful heart was actually a part of a shoe print in the sidewalk cement. I was so surprised. I could see both the heart and the shoe print. I love it!

I've recently learned that some of my heart-finds, the ones where I see hearts in various objects and patterns could be considered "pareidolia"—seeing familiar objects or patterns in otherwise random or unrelated objects or patterns. It reminds me of the notion that when we see or discover the beauty and positivity in things and circumstances, our lives can be more enjoyable and joyful. I'm all in for that!

"We don't see things the way they are.
We see them the way we are."

—Talmud

open hearts

Such an amazing way to start the New Year! I think this heart is the result of a mix of rain water and oil.

When I enlarged the photo, I got a better look at the heart's amazing prism of colors. So unique and gorgeous. Like so many of the other hearts I've shared with you, I believe it's a subtle way the universe is sending me a message on the first day of the year. It's confirming we all need to be present, open, and willing to receive its messages. Synchronicity!

"There are no coincidences, only synchronicities: mini miracles placed before us by the Angels with love to inspire the mind and expand the heart."

—Molly Friedenfeld

God's presence

Have you ever walked a certain route and thought you had noticed everything around you, but then one day you see something that had obviously always been there, and you are just noticing it for the first time?

That just happened to me; I discovered this beautiful heart that I hadn't seen before. I consider it not only a reminder of the Divine's presence in our lives, but of the importance of keen observation as well. Glimpses of the natural beauty in our surroundings are so comforting and uplifting, a calm contrast to the world's turmoil.

"Sometimes it is the quiet observer who sees the most."

—Kathryn L. Nelson

moment of joy

This incredible heart-find stopped me in my tracks while I was mowing the lawn. I rarely come across a rock or stone in our yard, so as you can imagine, it not only took me by surprise but gave me goosebumps.

I've always liked mowing the lawn. My current lawn mower, Ruby 3 (She's ruby red and my third one) is one of my treasured material possessions. Cutting the grass brings me so much joy, because it's one of the few things in life where I'm able to see my results right away.

While mowing, I often get lost in my thoughts. And for the past couple of years, my thoughts have tended to revolve around things that worry me. I try to redirect my thinking to things that make me happy or even sing a song to myself that puts a giddy-up in my step, but I'm not always successful. I wish I could be like those people who when asked what they're thinking, their response is "Nothing."

This heart-find brought me joy and helped me change my train of thought. It reminded me that there's always hope. I know in my heart things can work out. I just can't lose faith.

"Hope is a seed God plants in our hearts to remind us there are better things ahead."

—Holley Gerth

heart shift

I can't believe how many hearts crossed my path on the last day of February—truly unbelievable, but so needed! My mind had been busy second-guessing all my work over the past month, our heart month, instead of relishing in the shared joy. Coming across all these amazing hearts, especially this sparkly silver charm and beat-up twist tie forming a heart, made me realize how much I need to take more time to enjoy and cherish my intangible but valuable riches.

Yep, I can be so guilty of not treasuring the special moments in my life. Consider this: every day in February, I shared on social media my heart's joys and struggles along with some of the ornaments, home goods, and jewelry in my heart collection. On February 28, instead of basking in the positive feedback I received throughout the month, I found myself critiquing my work and thinking of ways I could have done a better job. My heart-finds reminded me the what-ifs and self-evaluations can come later.

"We can only be said to be alive in those moments when our hearts are conscious of our treasures."

—Thornton Wilder

renewed hope

It's the first full day of spring. Many of you know I'm a cold weather person, but I look forward to this beautiful season before the heavy heat and humidity settle in. I look at spring as the harbinger of renewal, hope, and growth.

It's always special for me to come across a heart when I'm out and about, and today's find is no exception. I see each one as a positive sign. As I say goodbye to our lovely winter, I welcome spring with a hopeful spirit.

> "Spring's first heartbeat honors winter's last breath."
> —Angie Welland-Crosby

my dad knew my heart

Although my dad lived 40 more years than my mom, when he passed, there were quite a few things between us that weighed heavily on my heart, things I never felt I could discuss with him. I wish I had the courage not to let my fear of upsetting him prevent me from broaching those sensitive subjects.

Although my gut enables me to believe my dad knew me and knew my heart, I'm still heartbroken and feel a deep remorse. I've been praying for signs that our relationship was the best it could have been given who he was and my respect for that.

And then look what appeared in my path today as I was walking from my car to the grocery store entrance. A cool piece of rusted metal shaped like a heart grabbed my attention. This timely heart-find gave me a closeness to my dad and a feeling of inner peace. Love you, DaddyO.

"The universe is full of magical things patiently waiting for our hearts to grow enough to see them."

—Frederick Backman

walking with grace

I go to our local Post Office on a regular basis to check my business mailbox. To my very pleasant surprise, I have come across some cool hearts from time to time. I often say to myself, "How did that get here?" or "Why haven't I seen that before?" Yesterday, I not only found this incredible heart, but as is often the case, it crossed my path when I really needed some hope and comfort. For sure, this heart-find appeared out of the blue at the most perfect time!

If we're fortunate enough for our parents to live a long, full life, many of us will go through challenging times as they age and their health declines. All kinds of issues can arise. I try my best to stay positive, but it's not easy. Such tugs on the heart can be so intense. I tend to want to fix things even though I know some, if not quite a few, of those things are out of my control. These challenging times occupy so many of my thoughts, especially when I'm by myself. This heart-find had a way of calming my heart and resting my mind. It reminded me of the Serenity Prayer's salient message and assured me things will be okay.

It's important to feel good about our efforts and realize there will always be things out of our control, but that doesn't mean those things can't still work out in due time.

"Incredible change happens in your life
when you decide to take control over
what you do have power over instead of
craving control over what you don't."
—Steve Maraboli

sign from above

I was in blissful disbelief that this silver metal charm was lying in the street right in front of our house. After picking up the pine cones in our yard, I had proceeded to the street to pick up a few more, and as I stepped off the sidewalk that goes from our house to the street, it was just lying there. Such an incredible find in a remarkable place. I believe in signs and this heart-find was one of the most obvious ones given its proximity to our home.

I stood on the street for what seemed like the longest time feeling so giddy inside and contemplating God's message to me.

I felt as though He was speaking to my heart, reassuring me that everything is going to be okay, I'm on the right path, and He is always with me. God is always speaking to us. We just need to pay attention to the signs he sends us.

"When you're going through a tough time, look for the signs that God is with you. He's always trying to reach out to you."

—Joyce Meyer

let love lead

Can you see the lovely heart my husband and I recently saw? With the help of some lush trees, the clouds formed a billowy heart. And it appeared at just the right time.

We were on the road to my in-laws' home to visit and help them with a variety of things. We were having a deep discussion about their needs—not an easy conversation— and this heart-find immediately lifted my spirits and served as a wonderful reminder: as difficult as family situations can be at times, it's so important that not only our minds but our hearts lead our thoughts and actions. We can't go wrong when we treat our loved ones with understanding, love, and kindness, just as we want to be treated.

"Try to be a rainbow in someone's cloud."

—Maya Angelou

close examination

As I go about my life, I'm always hoping and praying for the best and trying not to lose heart. It's not always easy, but it's helpful and comforting to have so many precious gems appear before me.

I can so relate to this newest heart-shaped rock and pretty much every single heart I've come across. Like me, none of them are perfect, nor do they pretend to be. They're a bit rough around the edges. And it's obvious they've been around for quite some time with a few scars to prove it. But all of the nicks and bruises can't be seen without an in-depth examination. I believe these scars also reveal character and resilience, having withstood what looks to have been multiple bumps in the road.

If we're really living our lives and not just going through the motions, we're going to get quite a few nicks and bruises. We have a choice as to how we deal with them.

"Life is not the way it is supposed to be. It is the way it is. The way you cope with it is what makes the difference."

—Virginia Satir

beauty in disguise

This heart-find is quite unique. When I first saw it, I thought it was a piece of tree bark. I loved its texture and different colors. So, I took a photo, carefully picked it up, and put it in my tissue which I gently placed in my coat pocket.

Well, guess what? This lovely heart, which crumbled in my tissue, was not bark from a tree. Before I even opened up the tissue, its smell gave it away. It was part of a mangled cigar. Nevertheless, it still made my heart happy.

"Beauty is not limited by our preconceived notions; it can be found in the most unexpected forms."

—Unknown

never alone

What a spectacular day as far as heart-finds go—I fatefully came across FIVE hearts, some nature-made and some man made. The last one I came across, shimmering in all its zirconium glory, was lying in a parking lot all by its lonesome. I can't help but think God and my angels are letting me know they have my back; everything is going to be alright.

We all need a sign from time to time, sometimes more often than others.

"If you have trouble hearing an angel's song with your ears, try listening with your heart."
—Terri Guillemets

Happy
Holidays

present and open

I can't help but feel good inside when I see that kids are still playing the same sidewalk games I played when I was a youngster so many moons ago.

I love this hopscotch court I came across a few days ago. I delighted in its holiday wishes and illustrations, but I especially loved that the illustrations included a heart. It made its message even more special.

During the holiday season, there is so much kindness in the air. Despite all the problems going on in the world, I can feel the love, care, concern, and appreciation everyone has for one another. Our hearts are more attuned to others, which, of course, is what I want all year round.

May our hearts always be present and open.

"The holiday season is a magical time when hearts open wider, smiles become brighter, and kindness prevails."

—Unknown

true friendship

I came upon this unique heart in a doctor's office parking lot the same day I had hesitatingly reached out to a trusted friend for some unfiltered constructive input on a challenging project I'd been working on for quite some time.

I was hesitant because it has always been hard for me to ask for help, and, admittedly, I was worried about what she would say about my work, even though I knew I wanted and needed her opinion.

This heart-find, which was embedded in the cement, is so amazing because it appears to have been formed by one stone clasping another. It's the embodiment of real friendship. Such a lovely sign and reminder of the importance of close friends supporting and encouraging each other. When we help each other, we contribute to each other's wholeness.

I thank my very special friend from the bottom of my heart.

"You can always find comfort in the hand and heart of a friend."

—Unknown

rooted resilience

This heart-find has such incredible character—it literally took my breath away when I came upon it. It's formed by the roots of an American Sycamore tree I've seen more times than I can count, but for some reason this is the first time its root system caught my eye.

God's beautiful creation reminds me of how our lives can be quite messy and stressful at times. Our scars, jagged edges, cracks, and crevices reflect many of our trials and tribulations. The more years we are blessed to live, the more visible the mess and stress become and the bigger impact they have on our heart and soul. They can make us bitter, or we can rise above and see beyond our circumstances to what really matters. It's our choice.

"Every test in our life makes us bitter or better, every problem comes to break us or make us. The choice is ours whether we become victim or victor."

—Unknown

trash to treasure

I stumbled upon these two heart-finds on different days, but I think they belong together. Both put a smile on my face, and one also gave me a good laugh.

The silver heart is a mangled gum wrapper. When I came upon the other one a couple of days later, I thought it had such a cool-looking texture. After I took a photo and began to pick it up, I realized it was a piece of chewed-up gum! Needless to say, I left it where I found it.

For sure, we can find hearts in all kinds of things, but what's so wonderful is how they make us feel when we spot them. They both lifted my mood and reminded me how the simplest of things can bring us joy. God is always with us and cares about us.

"The most simple things can bring the most happiness."

—Izabella Scorupco

held together

Do you ever feel like your heart is being held together by staples? I think it's normal to not always be on the same page with our family and friends. But there are times when a disagreement has hurt my heart more deeply than others.

At times like this, I've always clung to the belief that there would be a resolution. However, it appears I'm in a permanent impasse with one conflict I'm facing. So now, I embrace hope as a source of strength to do what is right for me. And I pray to God to help me heal and move on with my life.

For this heart to find me at this time in my life is incredible. It literally has staples all over it. With this newfound hope, I feel a sense of mending in my heart.

"Hope is a renewable resource."

—John Green

hope is everywhere

It's not unusual to find heart-shaped seashells on the beach, but that's not where I found this one. I was on foot, cutting through a high school running track, to get to a parking lot when this stunning shell jumped out at me.

Such an unexpected and beautiful heart-find gave me a big boost. I was absorbed in thought, admittedly more like worry, about family. And this heart-shaped seashell gave my brain and heart a different, positive focus. At that moment, I felt God was letting me know to never lose hope.

Hope can be found in the smallest of things in the least likely of places. When our hearts are open, we can hear the subtle whispers of God's guidance.

"Life can be full of unexpected things, either happy or sad. But no matter what happens, just keep a loving heart, a wise mind and a strong faith in God. He will always stay with us through all the journeys of our life."

—Unknown

faith forward

Lately, I've been feeling down, thinking about all the things going on with my family and work. I have found myself questioning why these things are all happening at the same time.

Finding this heart in the parking lot at this point in time gave me the boost and affirmation I really needed. I knew I had to get out of my head, stay faithful, and keep charging ahead.

I don't know if you can tell from the photo, but I'm quite sure this heart-find is a piece of ripped particle board that the wind blew into this parking lot. And like many of the other hearts I have found, it's by no means perfectly shaped, but its jagged uneven edges are what make it so beautiful and special.

We must never lose our faith and hope in what we're trying to accomplish in our personal and work lives. God is always with us, and it sure is comforting to be reminded from time to time.

"Every difficulty you face, in every waiting place, you're being given the chance to trust in the things unseen and to be abundantly blessed."

—Cherie Hill

celebrate change

I'm always ready for summer to give way to fall. I love what this upcoming season represents: a time for change and reflection, and, equally important for this snow lover, cooler temperatures.

As summer and fall collide, our neighborhood streets are a mix of the crape myrtles' faded flower petals and seed capsules and the pine trees' straw. And look what I found—such a fun heart—it looks like a celebration of the two seasons. Crape myrtle confetti!

God reminds us to always take the time to rejoice and reflect on our blessings as the seasons change. There is always hope and joy to look forward to.

"Autumn is the season of change, a time to reflect and to grow."
—Unknown

heart's key

All the hearts I find not only give me an indescribable lift but also make me self-reflect.

Look closely at this one. It appears to be a key, which made me think about the different keys to my heart. The special people in my life and sentimental objects have a way of unlocking my heart.

I got goosebumps when I found this cool heart-shaped key. It gave me a much-needed burst of energy and joy. Meaningful relationships restore my faith in humanity and warm my heart. Let's always be aware and appreciative of who and what touches our hearts. With this mindfulness, we will not only understand ourselves better but our connections to others will be deeper.

"The royal road
to a man's heart
is to talk to him about the
things he treasures most."
—Dale Carnegie

dreams realized

Have you ever had a time in your life when things were finally coming together, but because you felt as if you had to go through hell to get to that point, it was hard to believe that these things were finally working out?

That's my situation right now. It appears that all my efforts are beginning to pay off, but I'm scared to count on it.

On a cold rainy morning, I was a ball of mixed emotions. I was running on fumes, having stayed up to the wee hours making sure I did all I needed to do to keep one of my projects moving in the right direction.

Then this happens: As I was rushing to get to my husband's truck, his headlights shined brightly on a precious heart lying in the street where he happened to stop to pick me up. Its rough edges and blemishes are quite pronounced, and not until I picked it up, did I realize it was a piece of Styrofoam.

More importantly, it was in that moment that a calmness slowly came over me. I could feel God's presence. He was letting me know it's okay to feel positive and excited about this project. Like this timely heart-find's imperfections, my project has had its rough spots, but I realize there's no reason it can't come together.

We must never give up on our hopes and dreams!

"Faith that it's not always in your hands or things don't always go the way you planned, but you have to have faith that there is a plan for you, and you must follow your heart and believe in yourself no matter what."

—Martina McBride

peace at heart

If there was ever a sign of God's presence and assurance, I found one the night my father-in-law, who I affectionately called Daddy Worrell, passed away. My husband, sister-in-law, and I were blessed to be by his side.

As I watched him and intently listened to the sound of his heavy breathing, I can't explain it, but I got a feeling in my gut, a nudge I couldn't ignore, to ask the duty nurse about the sound. Following my concern, she contacted his hospice nurse. Upon returning, she advised us that it was best to remove his oxygen tube. He passed away peacefully within seconds.

As the three of us were leaving the hospital, shortly before midnight, there was no one at the reception desk. A computer screen was shining brightly with this most bold and beautiful heart from the heavens. My husband and sister-in-law had already passed by the desk. Both excitedly and nervously, I called out to them to come back and look at what I had found. Wearily they walked back to see what in the world I was talking about. They were just as amazed as I was.

I truly felt God was with the three of us, and I couldn't help but also believe He was letting me know we did the right thing for Daddy Worrell.

"God leads us. God will do the right thing at the right time. And what a difference that makes."

—Max Lucado

not alone

It never gets easy to lose a loved one, no matter how many times we face this inevitable part of life. With the recent passing of my father-in-law, I've been overwhelmed with sadness and haunted by "what if?" questions. And the estate matters add another layer of stress. My husband, sister-in-law, and I are doing the best we can.

Two days after the funeral, my husband and I took a little walk, and were engrossed in conversation, going over everything we've been through and everything we still need to do. And look what I found! A beautiful, albeit quite weathered, heart-shaped metal charm. I knew in that instant it was a message from God, letting us know everything was going to be okay; we would emotionally get through this and get everything done.

It's human to feel beat up like this precious gem when going through a huge loss, but there's such comfort and a deep sense of inner peace when we know we're not alone.

"No matter the challenges you are passing through today; always remember you are not alone."

—Abdulazeez Henry Musa

positive reinforcement

Springtime often means constant sniffles and nagging headaches for those of us who struggle with allergies. They keep me from fully embracing all of the season's beauty. But look what stopped me in my tracks while my husband and I were walking and having a deep discussion about our family matters. Such an ethereal heart created from the reflection of white clover.

It doesn't escape me how simple ground cover is making such a lovely heart. It's not only a wonderful reminder to be mindful and appreciative that we can soak in all of nature's beauty, but it also helps me redirect my thoughts and attention to the positive things in my life.

"I firmly believe that nature brings solace in all troubles."

—Anne Frank

my mom is always with me

I often think about my mom and regret with all my heart that her time on earth was cut so short. I find myself talking to her from time to time, sharing my personal thoughts and feelings. And I often wonder if she can hear me and if she's aware of all the important things that have happened in not just my life but everyone in the family since her passing.

This heart-find made me tear up. Sure, it's a very pretty charm, but what makes it even more beautiful for me is that my mother's name began with the letter M. My feelings in that instant are hard to put into words, but in that moment, I felt as if my mom was letting me know she's with me. The comfort and joy it gave me and continues to when it comes to mind or when I take a look at it from time to time is priceless. No doubt, it was a sign from up above that my mom, one of God's angels, hears me and knows my heart.

"There are no goodbyes for us. Wherever you are, you will always be in my heart."
—Mahatma Gandhi

Choose Happy

I can't deny I have doubts, fears, and anxieties. Shoot, I'm human. But then I choose to be mindful of all my blessings, to pay attention to the unexpected but oh so powerful signs from up above. And my heart is happy.

"The happy heart runs with the river, floats on the air, lifts to the music, soars with the eagle, hopes with the prayer."

—Maya Angelou

Acknowledgments

My love and unwavering gratitude go first to my parents, both of whom I miss immensely. They instilled in me the values of giving 100 percent in everything I do, never giving up, and living by The Golden Rule. These are lessons I carry with me always. I also truly appreciate my sisters. Their belief in me has been a significant source of strength and motivation. My stepmom's trust in my ability to get things done is most appreciated. And I'm forever grateful to my in-laws and sister-in-law who have always treated me as a daughter and a sister. They have always believed in me and supported all my endeavors.

I give my heartfelt thanks to my book angels, Joni Albrecht, Constance Costas, Wendy Daniel, and Cathy Plageman. You have helped make one of my biggest dreams come true and I'm forever grateful.

❤ ❤ ❤

Over my life, I've had the good fortune to cross paths with many individuals other than family who deserve credit for helping me with some aspect of my life, most often, unknowingly. Whether it be personal or work-related, their thoughtful attitudes and actions have touched my heart in a big way and positively impacted my course. They may have just been doing what comes naturally for them, but for me, it was so much more. They opened their hearts and minds for me and that has made a profound difference to me and my path. I hope they already know how much I appreciate them, but memorializing their names in this little book is another way to express my heartfelt appreciation. Thank you from the bottom of my heart!

❤ ❤ ❤

Ed Allen
Liz Atkinson
Wendy Auerbach
Mary Lou Baird*
Bonni Barron
Jay Bienkowski
Morris Blueford
Martha Broecker
Barb Brown

Sue Bucenell
Chris Buchanan
Pat Bunting
John Butenschoen*
Vernie Calkins
Marlo Calloway
Gail Caltrider
Peggy Carr
Chris Churchill

Sandy Conrad*
Tommy Craig
Frank Cucci
Keith Cullen
Tony DiClemente
Nadine Diggs
Ben Edwards
Wayne Enders
Tom Enright
Sue Fahey
Rick Flanigan*
Martha Fowlkes
Leslie Gallop
Dave Hannegan
Polly Hanson
Whitney Henry
Clay Hogue
Candy Holland*
Chris Hoye
John Hull*
Christina Koomen
George Kotarides
Lorraine Lerner
Brenda Lloyd
Robby Lloyd
Lucien Lombardo
Mike London
Arthur MacConochie*
Courtney Many
Carolyn Martin
Howard Mast*
Allen McCreight
Mike McDevitt
Michele McKinnon
Michael McMahon
Alex Mitchell
Dorothy Moore
Mark Morehouse
Sharon Mundie
Eileen Olds
Ken Overton

Karen Parker
Katy Pishko
Connie Raby
Laulie Richardson*
Nick Riggio
John Roache
Micky Roberts
Sharon Robidere
Ed Rogers
Joe Saiia
Angela Sanchez
Johnny Sancilio
Valerie Saunders
Dean Schmidt
Tommy Semler
Sandy Skeen
Lisa Skinner
Mike Skinner
Mary Smith
Samantha Soupene
Karen Spangenberg
Chantale Taylor
Tammy Taylor
Jane Terrill*
Phil Walzer
Mike Warren
Connie Waterbury
Anita Weaver
Dottie Wikan
Christopher Witherspoon

*Deceased

In her debut book, *HEARTS: Finding Unexpected Signs of Hope, Comfort, and Joy*, Roze Worrell explores the profound experience of connecting with God through the simple pleasure of seeing signs and seeking their meanings. Her fresh approach to the divine embraces  equal parts coincidence and providence. Her practical take-aways offer a guide to living well no matter the circumstance.

For fifteen years, Roze dispensed commonsense advice for common workplace problems through her trusted column, Workplace Woes—Roze Knows, which ran in The Virginian-Pilot and on ABC-TV affiliate websites.

Her workplace consultancy philosophy, H.E.A.R.T. (Honesty, Empathy, Adaptability, Responsibility, and Teamwork), was inspired by an intense outdoor survival course. Its foundational principles inform her approach to work, life, and writing.

Before becoming an author and small business owner, Roze worked for the Dow Chemical Company, Virginia Opera, and the FBI. She earned a B.A. in American Government from the University of Virginia and an M.A. in Humanities from Old Dominion University. Roze and her husband, Brad, live in Norfolk, VA, where she continues to write and speak about the heart, from the heart. To follow along, visit www.rozeworell.com.